The Byzan

The Eng.

Keith Goodman

Written by Keith Goodman

Reading Age for this book: 8+

The reading age for the series will vary but starts at seven

The English Reading Tree Series has been written for children aged seven and over. It is the perfect tool for parents to get their children into the habit of reading.

This book has been created to entertain and educate young minds and is packed with information, trivia, and lots of authentic images that bring the topic alive.

A quiz at the end tests how much has been learned.

TABLE OF CONTENTS

The Byzantine Empire

The colosseum in Rome is one of the great wonders of this civilisation

The Roman Empire lasted for around a thousand years and had a massive impact on ancient civilizations.

This impact can still be felt today and forms the basis of Western government, architecture, engineering and literature.

The Roman Empire marked a golden age in development, but when it ended, there was a massive split, and two empires emerged.

The Eastern Roman Empire turned into the Byzantine Empire, which lasted another thousand years, while the Western Roman Empire, centered in Rome, collapsed in 476 AD.

During medieval times (Middle Ages), the Byzantine Empire ruled most of Southern and Eastern Europe, and its capital was the fabulous city of Constantinople, the wealthiest city in the ancient world.

Timeline One of the Byzantine Empire

330 AD: Constantine changed the name of Byzantium to Constantinople, and it became the capital of the Roman Empire. Constantinople would eventually become the capital of the Byzantine Empire.

395 AD: The Roman Empire splits into two halves. Rome was the capital of the West and Constantinople the East.

476 AD: The Western Roman Empire falls, and the Eastern Empire is now called the Byzantine Empire.

The Founding of Constantinople

Old Constantinople

Constantinople is now known as Istanbul and is situated in modern-day Turkey.

Because of its excellent position, the city was founded by the Greeks and called Byzantium.

The Roman ruler Constantine renamed the city of Byzantium in 330 AD and called it after himself. Constantinople means the city of Constantine.

The Roman Empire was so vast that it became difficult to run and protect its borders. Lots of tribes moved into Roman territories and could not be stopped.

The empire was divided into two in 395 AD. The split changed the Roman Empire forever as now, there were two emperors and two empires that governed themselves independently.

Rome was the capital of the West.

Constantinople the East.

The Eastern Empire thrived, as did the city of Constantinople, which became rich and very powerful. The city was Christian, and because it was situated on a peninsular, it was easily defended against attack.

The Western and Eastern Empires thought of themselves as Roman and celebrated their Roman history. They were governed separately, but the form of government was similar and typically Roman.

It was inevitable that, over time, differences would become bigger.

The population spoke Roman in the West, but in the East, the main language was Greek. In Rome, the religion was Catholic, while in Constantinople, it was Eastern Orthodox.

The Western Empire was overrun by barbarian tribes and collapsed in 476 AD.

The Eastern Roman Empire eventually became known as the Byzantine Empire and continued for over one thousand years.

Timeline Two of the Byzantine Empire

526 AD: The reign of Justinian starts. Justinian re-conquered many parts of the Western Roman Empire and constructed the famous Hagia Sofia in Constantinople.

Justinian was the last emperor to be named Caesar.

610 AD: Heraclius became emperor.

726 AD: Emperor Leo III bans the use of icons

800 AD: Charlemagne was crowned in Rome by the Pope as Emperor of the Romans.

For the first time in 300 years, there is an emperor in the west and the east.

843 AD: The worship of icons was restored.

The Reign of Justinian

The Byzantine Empire (Eastern Roman) was one of the longest-lasting in history and, at its peak in the Middle Ages, was one of the wealthiest and most advanced.

The collapse of Rome was the beginning of the Dark Ages in Europe, but Constantinople and the Byzantine Empire flourished.

Justinian was born in Macedonia in 482 AD. He was not born into a wealthy family, and his mother was a peasant. However, his uncle was in the Imperial Guard and made sure that Justinian was well-educated. Justinian moved to Constantinople, and when the emperor died without an heir in 518, his uncle took the position of emperor.

Justinian became one of his uncle's advisers, and when he died in 527, Justinian seized power and declared himself the new emperor.

Justinian thought of himself as a Roman, as did most people who lived in the Byzantine Empire. He wanted to restore the power of Rome, and his armies successfully conquered much of the land lost in the Western Roman Empire. This included regaining Italy and the city of Rome.

Justinian loved religion and art, and during his reign, Christianity, poetry, and literature flourished. He built many churches, bridges and dams, but his most famous work was the construction of the Hagia Sophia in Constantinople. This cathedral (now a Mosque) is still one of the most magnificent buildings ever built.

Emperor Justinian died in 565 after ruling his empire for 40 years. He had no children, so his nephew Justin II took the throne.

Justin II inherited a large empire but was not as quick-witted and wise as his uncle. He started a war with his Persian neighbors (The Sassanid Empire), and Italy was overrun by the Lombard tribe from Germany. Large areas of land in the east were lost during the Sassanid War.

Emperor Heraclius

The main threat to the Byzantines came in the form of Islamic

warriors who conquered all before them

Heraclius became the Eastern Roman Emperor in 610 and started

to win back the land that Emperor Justin II had lost.

The armies of Heraclius attacked the Persians, and although they were initially defeated, the Romans beat the Persian forces at the Battle of Nineveh in 627. The Persians agreed to give back all of the territories they had taken, and peace was restored between the two empires.

However, a new threat proved to be more dangerous than the Persians. The Muslim forces swept through the east and conquered all before them. In less than 100 years, Muslim forces would conquer land from central Asia to Northern Spain.

This began what is known as the Byzantine Dark Ages and marked a time when the Byzantine Empire struggled to survive.

Many people within the empire thought that it was a punishment from God for worshipping golden idols.

A new religious policy was introduced in the hope that this would solve the military problems that they were facing.

This new religious policy was called Iconoclasm.

Iconoclasm

The cross was an accepted religious symbol for iconoclasts

The Bible warns us against using icons, and the iconoclasts seized upon this. These people within the Byzantine Empire believed you should not worship religious images.

Since the time of Emperor Justinian, images of Saints had become a widespread form of worship. Many people in the empire thought that icons had magical powers that would protect them. When the Persian Army attacked Constantinople in 626, images of Mary had been held up on the walls during the fighting. This was later claimed to have saved the city.

Some leaders of the Byzantine Empire became convinced that believing in the power of icons was against God, and because of this, Emperor Leo III banned the use of icons.

The religious argument continued over many years until, eventually, icons were allowed.

Empress Theodora restored worship using icons, and it is still in practice today in the Greek Orthodox Church.

Charlemagne

Charles I (Charlemagne) was one of the greatest and most successful kings in medieval times. He was King of the Franks but, in later life, became the Holy Roman Emperor.

He was born in Belgium in April 742. The Franks were a collection of warlike Germanic tribes who lived in what we now call France.

As King of the Franks, Charlemagne attacked and conquered nearby territories, expanding his kingdom into Germany. He also attacked Italy and captured Rome, moving onwards to Spain. Some parts of Spain became part of the Frankish Empire.

In 800 AD, Pope Leo III crowned him Emperor of the Romans, which meant there was once again an Eastern and Western Roman Empire.

Charlemagne died in Germany in January 814.

Timeline Three of the Byzantine Empire

976 AD: Basil II is crowned emperor

1054 AD: The Great Schism. The Catholic and the Greek Orthodox Church fall out.

1095: The First Crusade saw an army from the West at the gates of Constantinople.

1204 AD: The Fourth Crusade. Constantinople is captured.

1261 AD: Constantinople is recaptured, and the Byzantium Empire restored.

1453 AD: The fall of Constantinople and the end of the Byzantine Empire.

Emperor Basil II

Many Viking warriors joined the elite guard of the emperor

In 867 AD, Basil I founded the powerful Macedonian Dynasty, and this period is often called the Macedonian Renaissance Period because art and learning flourished. The collection and storage of knowledge during this period and the expansion of its borders made this a golden age for the Byzantine Empire.

Basil II expanded the empire towards the north and came into conflict with the powerful Bulgarian Empire. The Byzantine Empire also fought with the Kievan Rus (Ukraine, Belarus and Russia).

A battle at sea between Russia and the Byzantine navy saw the use of the Byzantine secret weapon. This was a substance known as Greek Fire, which could burn on water and destroy ships.

Eventually, the Rus (Russians) were converted to Christianity, and they developed an alphabet based on Greek. This was called the Cyrillic script and made it possible for them to write their own Bible.

The powerful Greek Orthodox Church had many differences from the Western Catholic Church based in Rome. These differences would soon lead to conflict.

The contact between the Byzantine Empire and Russia led many Vikings living in Russia to travel to Constantinople. These Vikings became an elite guard of future Byzantine Emperors.

Basil II died in 1025.

The Great Schism

The Great Schism took place in 1054 when the Christian Church was divided into two. There was the Catholic Church in the West and the Greek Orthodox Church in the East. Even though there have been several attempts at reconciliation throughout history, the differences between the Churches remain to this day.

The Great Schism is also called the East-West Schism. It happened in 1054, but the situation had been tense between the two Churches for a long time.

The word Schism means split. The split was about religion and politics and started when the Roman Empire was divided into two. The East and West gradually moved apart culturally. Latin was spoken in the West, while Greek was the primary language in the East.

The Churches began to have different views on religious ceremonies. These differences widened, and in 1054, the Churches separated. There are many differences between the Orthodox and Catholic Church:

1. Orthodox Christians believe that Jesus Christ is the head of the Church. The Roman Catholic Church has the Pope as its head.

2. Orthodox Priests grew beards because Jesus Christ had a beard.

3. The two Churches make the sign of the cross in different ways.

4. The way of praying in Church. Catholics kneel while an Orthodox congregation stands.

5 Orthodox priests can marry before being ordained

6 Performing Mass. The Churches use different bread

The First Crusade

In the eleventh century, the Byzantine Empire encountered the warlike Seljuk Turks, who overran land in the Middle East.

The Turkish leaders were not as easygoing as the Muslim Caliphate. The Turks began to attack the Byzantine Empire. They also stopped Western Christians from going on pilgrimages to the Holy City of Jerusalem.

The Byzantine Empire asked the Pope in Rome for help, and the Pope began to preach that they needed to rescue Jerusalem from the Turks.

The Pope said the Crusaders would go to heaven if they helped the Byzantine Empire and freed Jerusalem.

The first Crusade was successful, and the Crusaders took Jerusalem. A lot of land taken by the Turks was given back to the Byzantine Empire.

The Fourth Crusade

The Crusaders attack Constantinople

The Fourth Crusade took place between 1202 and 1204, but instead of capturing Jerusalem, the Christian Army conquered the Christian Byzantine Empire.

After the disastrous Third Crusade, the Pope in Rome called for a new one, and by 1201, an army had arrived at the Italian port of Venice.

It was agreed that the Venetians would transport the Crusaders to the Middle East. The Crusaders realized they could not afford to pay the Venetians, so they agreed to help them attack the Hungarian port of Zara, which used to be owned by the Venetians.

At Zara, the Crusaders were asked to help the deposed Byzantine Emperor Isaac II in return for money. The Crusaders set off for Constantinople rather than Jerusalem.

The Crusaders and the Venetians attacked and took the city of Constantinople in 2004, and much of the city's riches were either destroyed or taken back to Europe.

The Byzantine Empire was divided between the Crusaders and the Venetians, and the Latin Empire was established.

The Byzantine Empire was almost obliterated by the Crusaders and the Venetians.

The Byzantine Empire is Restored

The unity between the Orthodox Church and the Catholic Church didn't last very long

The Byzantine Empire rose again briefly when, in the year 1261, Emperor Michael VIII of the Greek Kingdom of Nicaea recaptured Constantinople. Michael founded the Palaeologos Dynasty, which would control the Byzantine Empire until the fall of its capital, Constantinople, in 1453. Emperor Michael was the first leader of the new Byzantine Empire.

Determined to stop his Christian neighbors from overrunning his Empire, Emperor Michael unified the Byzantine Orthodox Church with the Catholic Church for a brief period. However, he did this at a price, as many of his people would not accept the union and were willing to go to prison for their beliefs.

The Fall of the Byzantine Empire

Constantinople fell to the Ottoman Army.

The Byzantine Empire ended in 1453 when the Ottoman Army attacked Constantinople using canon and took control of the city. The last Emperor was Constantine XI, who died in battle defending his empire.

The fall of Constantinople marked the end of one of the greatest empires that the world had ever seen and also marked the beginning of the powerful Ottoman Empire that would dominate the Middle

East for centuries. The Ottoman Empire would also wage war against the Christian countries of Europe and spread Islamic doctrines to the people it conquered.

The destruction of the Byzantine Empire also marked the end of the Roman Empire, as the Byzantine people called themselves Roman, even though they spoke Greek. The Invasion and defeat by the Ottoman Army marked the end of a Roman Empire that stretched back to 27 BC.

Summary of the Byzantine Empire

Constantinople, is now modern-day Istanbul

The people of the Byzantine Empire called themselves Romans even though they spoke Greek and had a different Church. After the obliteration of the Western Roman Empire, the Eastern Roman Empire continued until it was finally defeated by the Ottoman Empire in 1453.

Most modern-day historians classify the Byzantine Empire as not being Roman but call it a medieval civilization.

When the Western Roman Empire fell, the Byzantine Empire became the most powerful state in the regions around the Mediterranean. However, with the rise of Islam, this power soon went into decline.

Even though Islam was a force that swept through the ancient world, the Byzantine Empire and Constantinople remained the center of great art and learning.

With the split between the Catholic Church and the Eastern Orthodox Church, there was, at times, deep hatred between the West and East. Despite the hatred, when the Seljuk Turks attacked Jerusalem, the Pope asked the leaders in Western Europe to raise an army and go on a Crusade to protect the faith.

The Crusades, however, would ultimately weaken the Byzantine Empire and leave it open to an attack by the Ottoman Empire in 1453. This marked the end of one of the longest and greatest empires that the world had ever seen.

Byzantine Empire Quiz

1 What city was the capital of the Byzantine Empire?

2 What city was the capital of the Western Roman Empire?

3 What was the main language spoken in the Byzantine Empire?

4 Which Emperor died in 565 AD after ruling for 40 years?

5 What religious policy banned the worship of icons?

6 What Byzantine secret weapon was used in a sea battle with Russia?

7 What religious event took place in 1054 and divided the Church into two?

8 Who attacked Constantinople in 2004?

9 Who briefly restored the Byzantine Empire in 1261?

10 What empire finally destroyed the Byzantine Empire in 1453?

Thank you for Reading this Book

You can visit the English Reading Tree Page by clicking:

Visit Amazon's Keith Goodman Page (Mailing List)

Books in the English Reading Tree Series by Keith Goodman include:

The Titanic for Kids

Shark Facts for Kids

Solar System Facts for Kids

Dinosaur Facts for Kids

Save the Titanic for Kids

Discovering Ancient Egypt for Kids

Native American Culture for Kids

The American Civil War Explained for Kids

The American Revolution Explained for Kids

World War One in Brief for Kids

World War Two Explained for Kids

Middle Ages Facts and Trivia for Kids

The Cold War Explained for Kids

The Great Depression and Stuff for Kids

Discovering Ancient Greece for Kids

The Vikings for Kids

The History of Ancient Weapons

Titanic Conspiracy Theories for Kids

The French Revolution Explained for Kids

The Bermuda Triangle Mystery for Kids

The Russian Revolution Explained for Kids

UFO Mysteries for Kids

Ancient Mesopotamia for Kids

Chinese Dynasties for Kids for Kids

Myths and Legends for Kids

The Loch Ness Monster for Kids

Ghost Stories for Kids

The Bigfoot Mystery for Kids

Unexplained Mysteries for Kids

The Vietnam War for Kids

The Knights Templar for Kids

The Crusades Explained for Kids

The Ancient Incas for Kids

World War One Planes for Kids

The Battle of Britain for Kids

The Byzantine Empire for Kids

Books in the Young Learner series

All About the Anglo-Saxons

All About the Titanic

All About the Battle of the Little Bighorn

All About the Second World War

All About the American Revolutionary War

All About American History

All About George Washington

All About the Normans

All About Japan

All About Stonehenge

All About Castles

All About the Hundred Years' War

All About World War Two Tanks

All About Queen Elizabeth II

Living History Series

1 Ancient Britain for Kids

2 Roman Britain for kids

3 Anglo-Saxon Britain for Kids

4 Viking Britain for Kids

5 Norman Britain for Kids

6 Plantagenet England for Kids

7 Tudor England for Kids

8 17th Century England for Kids

9 Georgian Britain for Kids

10 Victorian Britain for Kids

11 Britain at War for Kids

12 World War Two Britain for Kids

Quiz Answers

1 Constantinople

2 Rome

3 Greek

4 Justinian 1 (The Great)

5 Iconoclasm

6 Greek Fire

7 The Great Schism

8 The Crusaders and the Venetians

9 Emperor Michael VIII

10 The Ottoman Empire

Attributions

Colosseum Author WelcomeTeam2020 Standard licence
https://depositphotos.com/ ID 344067796

Egg-timer Author oleg_katya_yd Standard licence
https://depositphotos.com/ ID 109289092

Old Constantinople Author marzolino Standard licence
https://depositphotos.com/ ID 13295897

Egg-timer Author oleg_katya_yd Standard licence
https://depositphotos.com/ ID 109289092

Justinian Author Morphart Standard licence
https://depositphotos.com/ ID 13671640

Islamic warrior Author sketch-hand-drawing Standard licence
https://depositphotos.com/ ID 417816458

The Cross Author biblebox Standard licence
https://depositphotos.com/ ID 320888878

Charlemagne Author marzolino Standard licence
https://depositphotos.com/ ID 13304989

Egg-timer Author oleg_katya_yd Standard licence
https://depositphotos.com/ ID 109289092

Viking warrior Author Morphart Standard licence
https://depositphotos.com/ ID 218082578

Candles Author nikola31 Standard licence https://depositphotos.com/
ID 332957778

Knight on horseback Author vukkosticart Standard licence
https://depositphotos.com/ ID 552259530

Made in United States
Troutdale, OR
04/06/2025

30377219R00030